Spilling the

Joan of Arc

and the burning issues of the time

First published in 2000 by Miles Kelly Publishing,
Bardfield Centre, Great Bardfield, Essex CM7 4SL

Printed in Italy

ISBN 1-902947-63-0

24681097531

Cover design and illustration: Inc
Layout design: GardnerQuainton

Spilling the Beans on...

Joan of Arc

and the burning issues of the time

by Victoria Parker

Illustrations Mike Mosedale

About the Author

Victoria Parker graduated from Oxford with a degree in English Literature and Language. She has since worked on various childrens books, writing and editing both fiction and non-fiction titles.

Contents

Introduction	Go Get 'em, Girls	7
Chapter 1	Rowing Royals and Suffering Citizens	12
Chapter 2	The God Squad	24
Chapter 3	Tried and Tested	38
Chapter 4	Arise, Sir Joan!	48
Chapter 5	Joan's Predictions Come True… Well, Some of Them, Anyway!	63
Chapter 6	A Dirty Dungeon and a Dismal Death	80
Afterword	Sorry! We Made a Mistake	90

INTRODUCTION

Go Get 'em, Girls!

For ten points... who is the greatest female fighting heroine the world has ever seen?

Think hard.

No, harder than that...

Hmmm, Xena Warrior Princess. Not bad for a first guess. She's a dab-hand with a broadsword, she can outdo most men

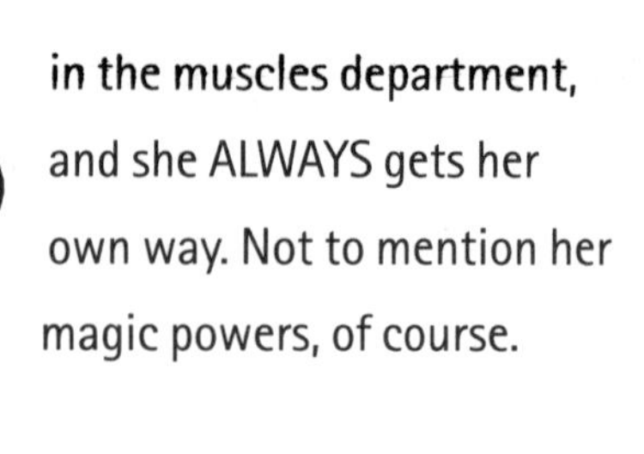

in the muscles department, and she ALWAYS gets her own way. Not to mention her magic powers, of course.

But not quite right, I'm afraid. No ten points. You'll have to think again...

Okay, Buffy the Vampire Slayer. Now you're getting warmer. Even if

you're the world's greatest Warrior Princess fan, you'd have to admit that sweet little Buffy outdoes big bad Xena every time. Even though Buffy's only half Xena's size and strength, she doesn't need the help of weapons. She just wipes out her enemies with her bare hands. With a toss of her long, perfectly blow-dried, blonde hair, she simply lets loose a few carefully placed punches, adds a somersault or two for good luck, and then high-kicks her victims into little piles of dust. And the bad guys aren't human – oh no, that would be too easy. They're supernatural!

But sorry… still no ten points. Have another go.

TING! Correct. Take ten points and have a bonus five because I'm feeling generous… **Joan of Arc** (also known as 'Joan the Maid' or 'the Maid of Orléans' or 'St Joan') is the female fighting heroine to top all female fighting heroines.

For a start, our Joan was a real person, not just a made-up character on the TV. This is, of course, a major advantage in the scoring, and more than balances out the face that 'Joan of Arc' isn't half as exotic or glamorous a name as 'Xena Warrior Princess' or 'Buffy the Vampire Slayer'.

Next, Joan was only 17 years old when she began her fighting career – even younger than Buffy. And she didn't just lead a gang of high school students; she inspired whole troops of French soldiers, defeated the English army in several important victories, and was the main reason why an heir to the French throne finally won his crown.

Finally, when it comes to the old 'magic' rating, Joan beats Xena and Buffy hands down. Inexplicable things happened to Joan her whole life long. She insisted that she heard heavenly voices and saw visions. She made several predictions that came true. She is said to have had amazing healing abilities. She also knew the whereabouts of a lost, sacred weapon that some believed was magic. (The story of how she came to possess her strange, ancient sword is even more mysterious than the tale of how King Arthur came to own Excalibur.)

Joan's strange powers were so extraordinary that she became famous far and wide – and many people became convinced that she was a witch...

There hasn't been a female fighting heroine like Joan of Arc since she was born over 500 years ago. Joan lived at a time when women were expected only to be housewives – whether you were a queen looking after your castle or a peasant looking after your hovel. So exactly how did a young village girl come to be the King of France's right-hand man (so to speak)? In the days before freedom fighters were even called freedom fighters, what did she do her freedom fighting for? And does her tale end happily, like all Xena and Buffy episodes?

If you want to find out more, this book will *Spill the Beans*...

CHAPTER ONE

Rowing Royals and Suffering Citizens

If you enjoy getting birthday cards and presents, stuffing your face with birthday cake, and playing mad birthday party games, thank your lucky stars you weren't born in medieval times. Birthdays were nowhere near as important then as they are now. Like many medieval people, Joan of Arc didn't even know exactly when hers was – although she thought she was probably born in 1412.

Now you might think that not having birthdays would make life pretty miserable. But I can assure you, in 14th- and early 15th-century France, that was the very least of the people's problems.

THE POPULATION TAKES A POUNDING

Between 1348 to 1350, the plague (also called the Black Death) swept across Europe inflicting a painful, messy death on hundreds of thousands of people. First, you'd have a headache and start throwing up. Then you'd shiver and sweat with a temperature. Big lumps the size of eggs would swell up in your neck, armpits and groin. Finally, gasping for breath, you'd turn purple and die. And you were extremely lucky if you escaped from it. According to a certain Henry Knighton:

> There died in Avignon in one day 1,312 persons, according to a count made for the Pope... And the sheep and cattle wandered about through the fields and among the crops, and there was no one to go after them or to collect them. They perished in countless numbers everywhere, in secluded ditches and hedges, for lack of watching, since there was such a lack of serfs and servants, that no one knew what he should do... The living did not suffice to bury the dead.

So many people died throughout Europe that landowners found that peasants were suddenly in very short supply. This was good news for your average European peasant and bad news for your average European landowner (well, those who survived, anyway!) because the landowners were forced to offer the peasants much higher wages than usual to get them to work on their land. But on top of this, French landowners and peasants had other problems to deal with, too...

WAR... WAR... AND MORE WAR!

The French had been at war with the English for 11 years before the Black Death struck, and the plague did nothing to stop it. The troops went on marching, camping and battling on French soil year after year, decade after decade. Coupled with the devastating effects of the Black Death, this crippled the countryside. The few peasant farmers who were left struggled to grow enough crops and rear sufficient livestock to feed the landowning lords and their soldiers, let alone themselves and their families. Even worse, bands of *ecorcheurs*, or 'skinners' roamed the country. These unemployed mercenary soldiers and bandits plundered towns and villages, stealing everything of value and burning anything else. Worst of all, the war showed no signs of stopping. By the time our heroine Joan was born in 1412, the war had been raging on French soil for a whopping 75 years!

KEEPING IT IN THE FAMILY

The seeds of all the trouble were really sown way back in 1066, when the French Duke William of Normandy defeated

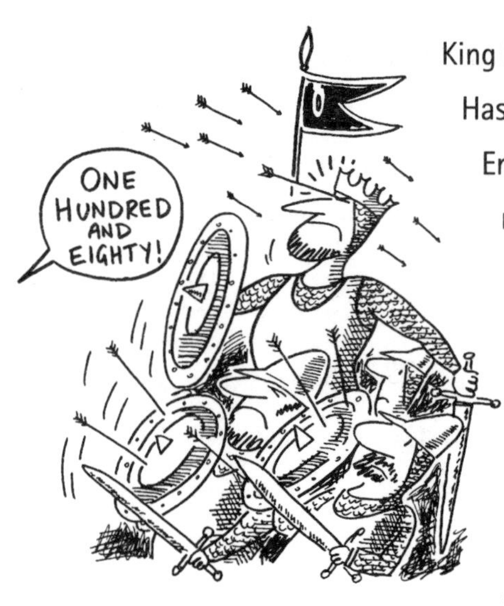

King Harold at the Battle of Hastings and claimed the English throne. (You remember the story – it was literally 'one in the eye' for poor old Harold.)

William the Conqueror (as he became known) drew England much closer to the Continent, particularly France (our prime minister today would have been proud of him). For instance, William gave much of England to the French lords who supported him. And French was even the language spoken at the English royal court for some years.

By the early 15th century, most of the French and English lords were closely related to each other. And they weren't any better behaved than families are today. They constantly bickered and fell out and fought amongst themselves – particularly over who was going to get all the money and property when a relative snuffed it. (And when I say 'fought', I really mean 'fought' – with armour and lances and swords.) When King Charles IV of France died in 1328, a huge family squabble broke out over who was going to get the French throne. Charles's cousin, Count Philip of Valois (who was French) and Charles's brother-in-law, King Edward III (of England), both claimed that they should be the next king of France. From a legal point of view, there wasn't much to choose between them. So Edward III wasn't at all happy when the Parlement of Paris decided that Philip should have the crown. In fact, Edward was so miffed, that in 1337, he went to war over it.

MADMEN, MALICIOUS MOTHERS, AND MAYHEM

The family squabble between the nobles turned into an international war between the English and the French that raged on for years – right into the next century. Year after year the fighting was fierce and bloody, but the French just managed to hold on to their crown. However, in the early 1400s, their fortunes began to take a turn for the worse. It began to look extremely likely that they would lose the throne to the English, for several reasons:

Reason 1

The Duke of Burgundy was the richest and most powerful of all the French lords. In 1407, he fell out with the Duke of Armagnac – another rich, powerful French lord (although not quite as rich and powerful as the Duke of Burgundy). As usual, the disagreeing dukes didn't just settle their differences with a scrap in the playground, they dragged their followers into it too. Their lands and armies were so big that this meant there was civil war within France. Now the French people were fighting each other, as well as the English.

Reason 2

The French king at the time, Charles VI, developed a mental illness and went totally mad. Everyone knew he could pop his clogs at any moment, leaving the throne up for grabs. The English heir at this time was King Henry V, who was bold and determined. He also had a huge army to back up his strong legal claim. Henry and his English forces had conquered a lot of French territory. He had even won the backing of some of the French nobles, including...

Reason 3

... the Duke of Burgundy (who, don't forget, was the richest and most powerful of all the French lords – a very good person to have on your side). This came about in 1416, when the Duke of Burgundy decided to side with his noble English relations across the Channel, rather than his French countrymen. (You've heard of the saying 'blood is thicker than water'?) The duke announced his support for Henry V and pledged that he and his Burgundian forces would fight for the English king. Together, the English and the Burgundians went on to occupy most of northern France – they even took Paris itself.

Reason 4

While the English claimant to the throne, Henry, was in a very strong position, the French claimant was in a very weak position. The French called their official heir the *Dauphin* (no, not the 'dolphin'), who was at this time the mad king's son, Charles. Well, at least the OFFICIAL position was that Charles was the mad king's son. In private, everyone had BIG doubts, because the queen had openly taken a lover – the mad king's brother, who was in fact much more likely to be Charles's dad than the mad king himself. This left big questions open over Charles's right to be Dauphin, and many of the snooty nobles in the French court looked down their noses at him. No one was 100 percent sure whether they should support him or not.

Reason 5

In 1419, Charles the Dauphin did something really stupid – he arranged the murder of the Duke of Burgundy (who, as you know, was fighting for Henry and the English). Firstly, this didn't do Charles any good, because the duke's son became the new Duke of Burgundy and took over just where his father had left off. Secondly, killing the richest and most powerful of all the French lords made Charles even more unpopular with the rest of the nobility. Worst of all, it REALLY annoyed his mother, the queen, because the Duke of Burgundy had been one of her best friends!

The queen paid her son back by agreeing to the Treaty of Troyes with the English. She signed away Charles's rights to the throne and agreed that on her mad husband's death, the French crown would DEFINITELY go to Henry V of England.

This was obviously a big kick in the teeth for Charles, and as you can imagine, he was extremely peeved. The few supporters the Dauphin still had left encouraged him not to take no for an answer. So Charles established a government-in-exile and tried to raise funds to pay for the French army to fight for him. Now, wars cost a lot of money, and after 83 years of fighting both sides were running short of cash. At one point, Charles was so skint that he had to sell the tapestries from his own walls to pay for his wedding! Even so, he managed to keep hold of some territories in southern France.

At last, in October 1422, the mad king died. King Henry V of England had died two months earlier, so after all that fighting he never got to be king of France anyway. But straight away, his baby son (another Henry) was proclaimed king instead – of both England AND France. As this was what had been legally agreed, no one publicly dared to argue with it – except for Charles the Dauphin, who stubbornly also declared himself king of France. So now France effectively had two kings – and the baby Henry VI held more territory than Charles did.

The French people themselves were split – they largely supported whoever held the territory in which they lived. So who knows how things might have turned out, if our Joan hadn't arrived on the scene to sort it out...

CHAPTER TWO

The God Squad

Quick question: Joan of Arc never existed – true or false?

a) True.

b) False.

c) Sort of.

If you answered **c)**, have 25 points.

There definitely was never anyone called 'Joan of Arc'. Our heroine was called 'Jhennette' when she was born, though her family called her just plain 'Jhenne' or 'Jeanne' as she grew up. (Spellings weren't as important in those days as they are now.) 'Jeanne' translates into English as 'Joan'. The 'of Arc' bit of her name wasn't given to Joan until at least 50 years after her death. Historians and poets made it up from the French *d'Arc*, which is a fancy, aristocratic-sounding interpretation of her father's surname, Darc. But in fact, even though Joan's father was a man of some local importance, he was far from aristocratic – he was just the keeper of the village cattle-pound! And besides, his surname might not even have been Darc at all. In the documents that tell of Joan, his name appears as Jacques Tart, Tarc, Dare and Day – as well as Jacques Darc!

However, we know that our heroine was definitely a real person, because there are a handful of surviving historical documents which tell us about her. We have three letters that Joan herself dictated (she couldn't read or write); letters from other people written about her; references to Joan in other chronicles of the time; and the records of her eventual trial and the investigations into it that followed.

HOME, SWEET HOME

Joan was born and brought up in a little village called Domrémy, which was split in half by the Moselle River. The houses on the east bank of the river were in territory held by the allies of the English, the Burgundians. The houses on the west bank of the river (including Joan's) were in territory held by the French forces of Charles the Dauphin. As Joan grew up, she got used to seeing the local lads coming back from the river all bloody from fighting with the boys on the other side.

Joan had to be careful not to venture too far into the fields when she was playing, for fear of bumping into marauding soldiers. So she spent a lot of time spinning and sewing at home with her mother, Isabelle – a very religious woman who inspired a deep love of God in her daughter.

POPE POWER

Joan's mother was a Catholic, because in medieval times, there weren't different Christian churches like the Church of England, the Baptists and the Methodists. All Christians were Catholics, and the Catholic church was (and still is today) told what to do by the Pope in Rome. Of course, the medieval kings and queens of Europe were Catholic too, so they also had to obey the Pope (often much to their annoyance). For instance, in 1095 Pope Urban II asked for the European royals to send knights to go to Jerusalem to throw out the Turkish rulers (who were Muslim). This started off a whole series of holy wars called the Crusades, which used up loads of the kings' time, money and best nobles (most of the knights were captured or killed by the Turks and never came back). King Richard the Lionheart of England was away so long on one Crusade that his subjects must have almost forgotten who he was...

In theory, the Pope was the most important person in Europe. Massive, magnificent stone cathedrals were built in the 12th and

13th centuries that rivalled and often bettered royal strongholds. And under the Pope, the Catholic church had the power to make laws and recommend that people were punished if they broke them. As Pope Boniface VIII wrote in 1302:

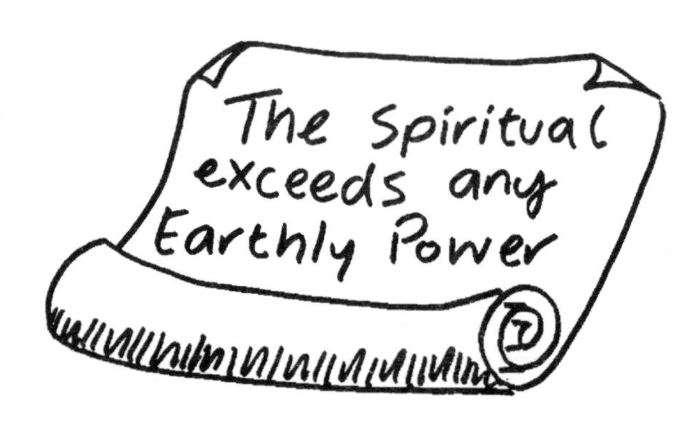

All this of course meant that kings and their laws came a definite second – which the kings often found to be a right royal pain. Archbishop Thomas à Becket reminded King Henry II of England about this in a letter in 1166. Becket wrote: '... it is certain that kings receive their power from the Church... so you have not the power to give rules to bishops'. Henry II was so cross that he had Becket promptly murdered in his own cathedral.

But even though the kings often got fed up about being ruled over by the Pope, they did get one benefit out of being part of the Catholic church – a pretty BIG benefit, in fact. Everyone believed that kings were appointed by God (the 'divine right of kings') and that they ruled with God's authority. Which made it very hard for anyone to criticize what they did.

This also made it even more confusing in early 15th century France to decide who should have the throne – the baby Henry VI or Charles the Dauphin.

Which is exactly why Joan of Arc was so important...

AM I SEEING THINGS?

One summer's day in 1425, when Joan was about 13 years old, she heard a voice and saw a light coming from the right-hand side of her village church. This was the first of many times

Joan heard voices speaking to her, and she later saw visions of St Michael the Archangel, St Catherine and St Margaret, too. The earliest message Joan heard was: 'Be a good girl and God will help you'. But as the months went on, the voices became more urgent. They told Joan that:

- She must go to the help of Charles the Dauphin.
- She should lead the Dauphin's forces in lifting the siege of the mighty city of Orléans.
- She should conduct Charles to a proper coronation at Rheims cathedral (where he would be anointed the true king with the special holy oil that was kept there).
- She should drive the English back to their own country.

Phew! Pretty daunting demands for a young, uneducated country girl. Yet Joan was convinced that the voices came from God and she should obey them. She had no doubt that

God meant Charles the Dauphin, not Henry VI, to be the king of France.

SUPER-CELEBRITY SAINTS

Medieval people were into saints in a big way. Everyone who was anyone had to have a bit of a dead saint – called a relic. People boasted that they had saints' bones, teeth and hair; cloth from Our Lady's robe; wood from baby Jesus's manger – even the whole head of John the Baptist! Today, the most famous relic is a piece of material called the Turin Shroud – people have only just recently decided that Jesus's body couldn't have been wrapped in it. It was the same with medieval relics – no one could tell whether or not they were fakes (and of course, most of them were). But they were taken very seriously. People went to great lengths to get their hands on them – whether it was by stealing them or paying for them. And relics were such big business that there were plenty of fraudsters who had them on offer – after all, how was anyone to know that they were walking round with a pig bone instead of St Peter's kneecap?

Some people today believe that if you only pray hard enough, certain saints can protect you or work particular miracles for you. But in medieval Europe, EVERYONE believed this. The best saints to put your money on were the Fourteen Holy Helpers, who were particularly popular from the 14th century onwards.

Now imagine you are a medieval French peasant (wearing your oldest, dirtiest, smelliest clothes might help with this). Can you match the following Holy Helpers to the list of favours that you might need to pray for on the opposite page?

1. St Barbara
2. St Blaise
3. St Christopher
4. St Cyriac
5. St Denis
6. St Erasmus
7. St Eustace
8. St George
9. St Giles

10. St Pantaleon

11. St Vitus

A. Help for mad people, people who had fits, and people who couldn't have babies.

B. Protection against lightning, fire and sudden death

C. Help for hunters.

D. Protection for travellers.

E. To cure fits.

F. To cure headaches and rabies (a type of illness you can catch from mad dogs).

G. Protection against demons and evil spirits.

H. To cure tuberculosis (a horrible type of chest infection).

I. To cure colic and cramp.

J. To cure sore throats.

K. Protection for soldiers.

Answers:

1. B **2.** J **3.** D **4.** G **5.** F **6.** I **7.** C **8.** K **9.** A **10.** H **11.** E

The remaining three Holy Helpers were St Achatius, who for some reason didn't have any particular job, and Joan's favourites: St Catherine and St Margaret.

According to tradition, St Catherine was a Christian who lived in Alexandria in the late 3rd century – which was very unlucky, because the then Emperor, Maxentius, ordered all Christians who lived in Alexandria to be killed. Catherine argued her case for believing in God so well that she convinced 50 judges (who Maxentius had put to death immediately for being foolish) and also won over Maxentius himself – who fell in love with her. When Catherine knocked him back, saying that she was in love with Christ, Maxentius didn't take it very well. He had Catherine tortured on a contraption of wheels and knives (from which the firework 'Catherine wheel' takes its name). Not content, he then had her beheaded.

In the 15th century, St Catherine was probably the best-loved saint of the day. She was the patron saint of philosophers and students – and of course, wheelwrights! She stood for independence and courage, and was an especial favourite for young, unmarried women – like Joan.

There are several versions of St Margaret's legend:

- She is said to have disguised herself as a man and lived in a monastery as a monk called Pelagius – until she was accused by another woman of being the father of her baby! Rather than revealing she was a woman, Margaret suffered in silence and was punished by living in solitary confinement on bread and water for the rest of her life. She only owned up to being a woman on her deathbed! (This wasn't as unusual as you may think. Several other female saints disguised themselves as men and ran off to live in monasteries, such as St Euphrosyne, who died in 470 after living for 38 years as a monk called Smaragdus.)

- In another version of Margaret's story, she was swallowed by a dragon and then born again out of its belly, totally unharmed. This made her the patron saint of pregnant women.

- Margaret is also said to have seen visions of Satan. This made her a good saint for people to pray to if they wanted help for those possessed by the devil.

- Margaret was also meant to have been dead against marriage – literally, as it turned out, because like St Catherine, in yet another version of her story she was tortured and killed for her vow of singledom.

St Michael the Archangel was another favourite saint in Joan's day – especially with knights, as he was always shown with armour and a sword, having battled the devil and won. This warrior saint was particularly popular in France, and he had been the patron of soldiers from Normandy when they conquered England and during the Crusades. 'Michael' is 'Michel' in French, and the monastery in northern France called Mont St Michel was a favourite destination for pilgrims in the 14th and 15th centuries. Even mad King Charles VI went there in 1394 in the hope of curing his madness, and because he got a little better for a while, he named his daughter 'Michelle' as a thankyou. Charles the Dauphin made St Michael even more trendy. When in 1419 the English got hold of an

abbey named after St Denis, the patron saint of France, Charles gave St Denis the sack and had St Michael painted on his soldiers' standards instead!

Of course, there's no way of ever proving that Joan's voices really were saints speaking to her. But Joan certainly believed whole-heartedly that they were. Later on, you'll find out just how much she trusted in them...

CHAPTER THREE

Tried and Tested

Joan's first problem was how on earth to get close to the Dauphin. Joan knew that her father would be furious if she went off with Charles's troops. Everyone viewed the women who rode pillion behind soldiers as little more than prostitutes. In fact, Joan's father once warned that he'd rather his three sons drowned his two daughters than have the girls become camp followers. (Sounds like a nice man!) So Joan ran away to stay with her older cousin, Durand Laxart, and begged him to take her to the provincial governor, Captain Robert de Baudricourt, in his mighty castle at Vaucouleurs.

Joan's first audience with de Baudricourt didn't exactly go very well. When the young peasant girl told the powerful captain that God wanted him to send her to the Dauphin, de Baudricourt simply told Laxart to send Joan back to her father with a smacked bottom! But Joan didn't give up. She tried again... and again... and even once set off on her own to see the Dauphin. (She turned back before she got very far because she decided that she wasn't going about things the way her voices wanted her to.)

While Joan was waiting for things to work out, her voices told her one day that the French had lost a very important battle for the city of Orléans. In turn, she told de Baudricourt of the defeat and warned him that if he hung about much longer, it would be too late.

After de Baudricourt found out that Joan's news was true, he seemed much more keen to send her to the Dauphin. (Surprise, surprise!) Mind you, he got a priest to check she wasn't possessed by the devil, first! Luckily, Joan passed the test. Finally, it was time to go!

WE'RE OFF TO SEE THE DAUPHIN...

Today, it's only old stick-in-the-mud fuddy-duddies who mind girls wearing trousers instead of skirts. And few people raise an eyebrow if they see a girl dressed as a boy or a boy dressed as a girl – it happens all the time on the Jerry Springer TV show! But in medieval times, if this sort of thing went on at all, it only ever went on behind closed doors. Medieval people thought that 'cross-dressing' was truly outrageous. In fact, it was a sin against church rules. Nevertheless, Joan decided that she would go and see the Dauphin dressed as a boy. Her voices told her to do it – and in any case, it was safer that way. The journey was going to be through territory swarming with dangerous bandits and soldiers who didn't exactly act like 'gentlemen' when they came across ladies. No one could argue with the common sense of Joan's disguise. So she borrowed some of her cousin's clothes and had her hair cut short and up over her ears, like a man. Little did Joan know at the time that this was going to get her into BIG trouble later on...

A SIGN OF THE TIMES

At last Joan arrived at the royal court at Chinon. And she soon found out that de Baudricourt's test was only the first of several tests she had to face...

Test number one

Joan had to convince the Dauphin that she really had come with God's blessing and that he really was God's chosen heir to the French throne. To do that, she needed to provide the Dauphin with a miraculous sign that could only be from God himself. To this day, no one knows exactly what this 'sign' was, but there are several theories:

- It's been said that the Dauphin tried to expose Joan as a fake by hiding behind his courtiers and putting someone else on his throne in his place. But this dastardly trick didn't fool the 17-year-old country girl. Even though she had never seen Charles before, she apparently turned away from the impostor, marched straight into the crowd, and knelt before the real Dauphin. For many people, this was proof enough that Joan was really receiving messages from God. However, other people still weren't convinced. After all, Charles was notoriously pot ugly. He was reported to have had a bulbous nose, a drooping lip, and to have been generally 'the ugliest man in Christendom'. With these kind of looks, surely it would have been hard to miss him!

- Other reports say that Joan prayed and a host of angels appeared, bringing the Dauphin a golden crown – a vision which it was said that 300 or so of the courtiers saw as well!

- Another theory has it that Joan had a private conversation with the Dauphin and told him that she knew all about a secret prayer he had made one night in his bedchamber. As the story goes, Charles had asked God that, if he wasn't the true son of the mad King Charles VI, he might be allowed to escape from France and live safely somewhere else. The fact that Joan knew all about this apparently got rid of all Charles's fears about his dodgy parentage and reassured him that he was the rightful king of France.

MAID OF HONOUR

Now Prince Naseem Hamed isn't a real prince, is he? And 'Posh Spice' isn't Victoria Beckham's real name either, is it? Many people change their names to help create an 'image' for themselves when they want to be publicly recognized and become famous. And Joan did just the same. When she introduced herself to the Dauphin, she called herself 'Jeanne la Pucelle', which translates into English as 'Joan the Virgin' or 'Joan the Maid'. It may be hard for us in the 21st century to understand why it would be important for anyone to be famous for not having a boyfriend. But for Joan, it was vital.

It's only over the past 100 years or so that people in the Western World have begun to see women as equally important to men. In fact, some people would argue that men are still thought in many ways to be better than women. But in medieval times, the situation for women was a million times worse than now. The medieval church actively taught that women's bodies were shameful and sinful. It spread the belief that it was by falling in love with women that men were dragged down into sin. Odo of Cluny wrote in the 12th century: 'To embrace a woman is to embrace a sack of manure'!

For this reason, women who didn't have boyfriends or husbands were thought to be pure and holy. Everyone believed that there was no way the devil could have anything to do with a woman who was a virgin. So Charles the Dauphin made Joan go for...

Test number two

Joan had to undergo a physical examination by Charles's mother-in-law and some of her ladies-in-waiting to check that Joan had never slept with a man. None of the women were trained medical people...

... but luckily, somehow, they were satisfied that Joan really was a 'maid'. For many people, the fact that Joan was as pure as Christ's mother, the Virgin Mary, was proof enough that her messages really were holy. Unluckily for poor Joan, Charles himself STILL wasn't quite 100 percent sure...

UNIVERSITY CHALLENGE

The Dauphin sent Joan to Poitiers, where he had gathered a university of learned theology and law professors, in an attempt to rival the English-controlled University of Paris. It was time for...

Test number three

For three whole weeks, the wise old men bombarded the 17-year-old country girl with questions about her background – particularly her voices, her visions, and her prophecies. Unfortunately, the records of Joan's examination at Poitiers no longer exist. However, we think that she made four predictions:

- The English would be defeated at Orléans and the besieged city rescued.

- Charles would be properly anointed king at Rheims cathedral.

- Paris would be taken back from the English.

- The Duke of Orléans would return from England.

The upshot of the examination must have been that the professors believed Joan was telling the truth. For at the end of it, Charles equipped Joan as a fully-fledged knight and sent her off to war!

CHAPTER FOUR

Arise, Sir Joan!

Joan was in fact never officially 'dubbed' or given a knight's title – even though Charles later honoured her brothers, who appear to have done nothing much at all, with the aristocratic name 'du Lys'. (That's medieval justice for you!) However, the king did kit Joan out with the full knight's regalia – an extremely expensive business! Charles ended up paying for Joan to have:

A squire

All knights had to have their own squire. These were trainee knights who acted a bit like golf caddies do today – running around after their boss, fetching and carrying, cleaning and polishing, and generally being helpful. If you were lucky, and more importantly could afford to buy your own weapons, you one day got to be dubbed a proper knight yourself – then it was your turn to boss someone else about and you could get your own back. Joan's squire was a man called Jean d'Aulon, who remained faithful to her through thick and thin.

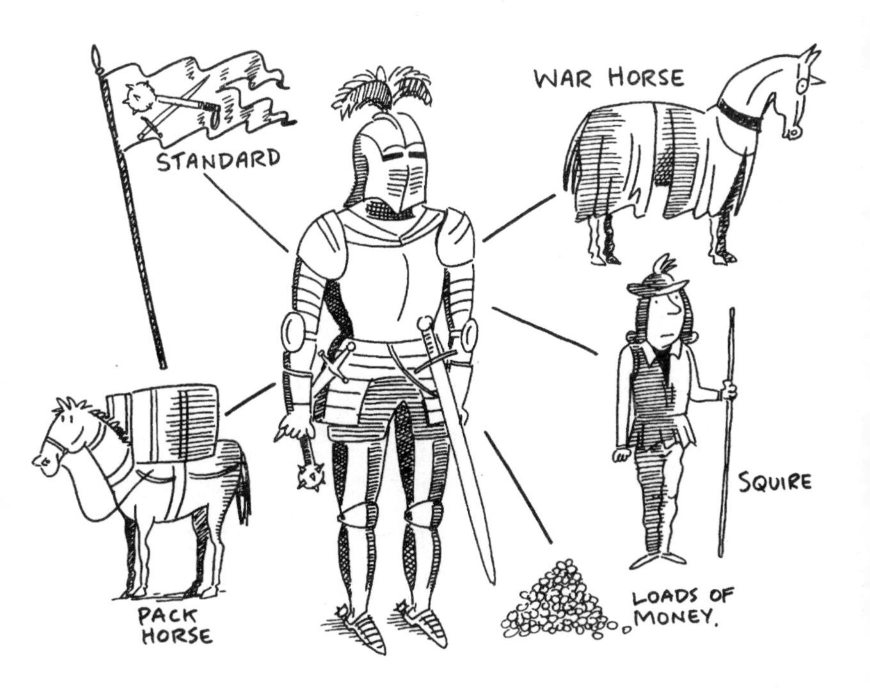

A suit of white armour

The very first knights had fought each other with lances and swords and worn chain mail for protection. But when the longbow was invented in the early 1200s, they found the arrows often went straight through – and who wants to look or feel like a pin-cushion? So safety-conscious knights started a new fashion – wearing 'plates' of armour over the most vulnerable parts of their bodies. By the mid-1300s, all canny knights ('canny' – get it?) were wearing whole suits of plate armour. These may have been incredibly uncomfortable (Joan slept in hers at first, to get used to it!) but at least knights stood more of a chance of staying alive.

Five warhorses and seven pack-ponies

Good horses were extremely expensive. But a knight didn't just need a brave, handsome horse to look the part at tournaments and win admiring sighs from all the ladies! A fearless, fast charger could mean the difference between life and death in battle. Sometimes horses were even taught to do their own fighting with their teeth and hooves. And a dead horse could always be fired over the walls of a castle on a catapult to attract lots of flies and germs into the enemy camp – hopefully also squashing some of the enemy as it landed!

A standard

All knights had their own family 'colours' or 'heraldry' – a design which told everybody at a glance who they were. (A bit like football team strips, really.) The designs were painted onto standards, or flags – and it was all very useful in battle. Firstly, all this marked out where your lot were, so you didn't end up attacking your mates. And secondly, it told the enemy whether it was worth keeping you alive or not – if you were from a rich family, you could be ransomed back for lots of money (as lots of knights were). Knights always chose pictures which they thought said a lot about them. Lions and dragons were always popular, although there were some very odd choices too – like porcupines and apples! Joan had a very fancy-schmancy standard. Her voices told her what to have on it: Christ holding the world between the angels Michael and Gabriel, above embroidered fleurs-de-lys (flowers which stood for France and the king) and the words 'Jesus Maria'.

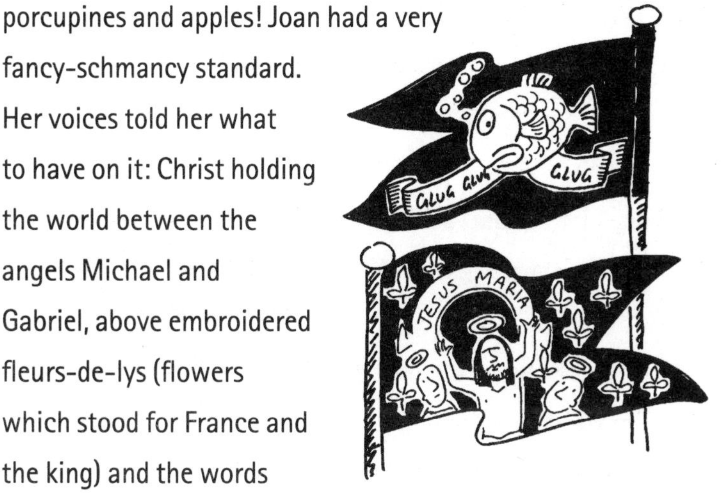

Off-duty outfits

When Joan wasn't in her armour, she didn't dress in women's clothes. She still dressed like a man, in a hose and doublet, with a jaunty hat on her head. Her clothes were posh and expensive, made of cloth of gold and silk and fur. Fashions were very important to rich medieval people. Like celebrities today, nobles saw it as part of their job to show off how many lovely designer clothes they had. But in the 14th and 15th century fashions got very silly, as nobles tried to outdo each other. And it wasn't just ladies who wore over-the-top clothes – lords did it too! Everyone could put up with women wearing daft things – after all, they were women, they were meant to be foolish! But lots of people warned against men following fashions. Not only was it sinful to love luxury, but the lords' huge, heavy costumes made it very difficult to run away from enemies! Some of the silliest fashions were:

- Long, pointy 'winkle-picker' shoes. (Some were so long and pointy that a chain was fastened to the tip, so the wearer could hold them up when they walked to avoid tripping over!)

- Long, pointy sleeves. (Some dangled right down to the floor and must have got very dirty – nice!)

- Long, pointy men's gowns and women's skirts. (Some trains

were so long and heavy that women needed pages to follow them around all day holding them up!)

• Long, pointy hats. (Queen Isabella of Bavaria had to have her doorways made higher because hers was so tall!)

THE SWORD UNDER THE STONE

The only thing that Charles didn't equip Joan with was a sword. He didn't need to – she had found one herself. Joan's voices had told her to send a messenger to a tiny chapel where supposed relics of St Catherine were kept. As instructed, the messenger dug behind the altar – and discovered an ancient sword, obviously from the Crusades, that no one had any idea was there... Sends shivers down your spine, doesn't it? The tales of the girl-knight and her 'magic' sword certainly terrified the English!

NASTY KNIGHTS

When Joan found herself at last being taken seriously as a soldier, she must have been delighted. But don't get the wrong idea – not everyone was as happy about it. In fact, most of Charles's favourites were extremely UNhappy about the way the Dauphin was making a fool of himself by listening to an uneducated peasant girl. And most of Charles's main men were far from the chivalrous knights they should have been. In fact, Joan was right in the middle of a very motley crew...

- La Tremoille had been Charles's first advisor – until Joan came along and pushed him out of the way. So naturally, La Tremoille hated her right from the start. And he wasn't a man you'd want to have as your enemy. He had a reputation for murder, blackmail and highway robbery!

- Gilles de Rais was the original 'Bluebeard' of the fairytale – a ruthless cut-throat who was later hanged as an alleged sorcerer and mass murderer.

- Arthur, Duke of Richmond, (or 'Richemont', as the French called him) was an English man who went over to Charles's side when he failed to get a good job in the English army! He also had two of Charles's closest friends murdered – not that Charles seemed to mind too much!

- La Hire was a very good soldier, but a very bad knight. In fact, he was little more than a bandit. La Hire once went to stay with a lord in his castle, then threw his host into his own dungeon and refused to let him go until the lord gave him lots of gold, wine and a horse! All this of course went right against the 'fair-play' rules of chivalry...

So these were the type of men that little Joan found herself up against, when she was trying to make the Dauphin follow the advice of her voices. She had an enormous job on her hands, and the fact that the grim leaders of Charles's court listened to her at all shows just how amazing Joan must have been.

JOAN HITS THE HEADLINES

Joan had one big thing on her side – fame. From the minute Joan had first gone to see Robert de Baudricourt, news had begun to leak out that there was a young girl going around saying that she had been sent by God to fight for Charles the

Dauphin. If they had had newspapers in those days, Joan would soon have been splattered across the front pages...

MAID TO MEASURE – GIRL SAYS SHE'S JUST THE JOB!

You can imagine how the secret got out – one of de Baudricourt's servants probably told his wife, who told her sister, who told the blacksmith's brother, who told his friends down the local tavern... and before you could say "Prophets alive!", everyone was talking about Joan and wanting to hear more about her.

EXCLUSIVE

I KNOW JOAN'S NEXT-DOOR NEIGHBOUR'S TAILOR'S SECOND COUSIN!

An in-depth article on the stunning young visionary!

By the time Joan had seen Charles, 'miraculously' recognized him, given him her heaven-sent predictions, and claimed her mysterious sword – even the English troops had heard the gossip.

FRENCH BRING OUT SECRET WEAPON – MAGICAL MAID OF MYSTERY!

The French public acclaimed Joan as an amazing young visionary who had been sent by the Lord and was going to save their war-torn country...

GIRL FROM GOD PROMISES FRANCE WILL BE FREE!

Faith in fortune teller grows daily

HOLY OR A HOAX?

Although there are some people today who claim to hear heavenly voices and see visions, there aren't many. Most of those that do end up either being given their own ratings-winning TV show or being locked away in a mental hospital. As for those who say they believe in someone who professes to have strange powers, well – they're usually mocked for it. (Remember how Glen Hoddle's belief in a faith-healer was one of the reasons why he lost his job as manager of the England footie squad? Mind you, perhaps people wouldn't have been so harsh if Hoddle's side had ever won anything... !) But back in medieval times, visionaries seemed to crop up much more often than they do now. Three of the most famous were:

- Elizabeth of Shonau (died in 1164), who had visions of the Virgin Mary and wrote essays warning women about the sinfulness of loving luxury.

- Hildegard of Bingen (died in 1178) – an accomplished scientist who also had heavenly visions from the age of five. She was later made a saint.

- Margery Kempe (born around 1373). She was a wife and mother who, after having visions and hearing voices, dedicated her life to God and took a vow never to sleep with her husband again.

As you can see, medieval people were used to their visionaries being women. Then again, being a prophetess was probably just about the only way that medieval women could get their domineering men to listen to their ideas and opinions.

Whether the visionaries were female or male, medieval people took them much more seriously than people do today. In fact, you could say that visionaries were the medieval equivalent of Hollywood stars. For instance, in the early 15th century, when a visionary called Vincent Ferrer visited Lyon, so many people flocked to see him that they went to the trouble of knocking down a wall so everyone could get a clear view. Not even Leonardo di Caprio has had to have that done for his fans!

Luckily for Joan, the medieval French royals were particularly keen on consulting fortune-tellers (a bit like our very own royals Fergie, the Duchess of York and the late Princess Diana).

- Before Joan was born, King Charles VI regularly asked for the opinions of a prophetess called Marie d'Avignon, and his wife, Queen Isabella, kept a visionary called Marie de Maille at her beck and call.

- A visionary nun called Colette lived at the same time as Joan. After the mother of the Duke of Burgundy met Colette in 1406, she took her advice for the rest of her life.

- Before Joan came onto the scene, Charles the Dauphin consulted a famous visionary called the hermit of St Claude. The hermit gave him two predictions: firstly, that Henry V would soon die; and secondly, that Charles would have a son. (The hermit turned out to be right on both counts.)

- The French courtly tradition of believing in visionaries was so strong that it continued well after Joan's life. Charles's son, Louis XI, kept the holyman Denis the Carthusian at his court. And once when Louis was very ill, he summoned the hermit Fra Roberto of Calabria in the hope that the hermit could heal him.

ABRACADABRA!

However, being an ultra-fashionable prophetess wasn't the only reason why Joan became so popular with the public, so quickly. On top of that, the men and women of France were actually *expecting* a female visionary to appear and save them. There had long been a folk legend about a mysterious woman warrior who would one day put an end to France's troubles. No one knew quite where the idea had some from. Some people thought the prediction had first been made over 500 years ago by the famous monk Bede, or King Arthur's wizard, Merlin. But by the time Joan arrived on the scene, new rumours had revived the old prophecy. It was said that the prophetess Marie d'Avignon had had a recent vision that the female fighting heroine was about to show herself.

In the light of all this, even Charles's tough, thuggish advisors had to admit that perhaps Joan's arrival at court was meant to be. Still, they didn't like it much. And many of them made up their minds to keep her out of things as much as possible...

CHAPTER FIVE

Joan's Predictions Come True… Well, Some of Them, Anyway!

If TV had been around in Joan's day, news companies world-wide would have sent their top war reporters to cover the action. The French evening news might have sounded something like this…

28 April 1429

I am speaking to you LIVE from the French army camp outside the besieged city of Orléans. The soldiers have been sent to try and save the starving citizens locked inside. It's probably the most dangerous place in the whole of the country at the moment. The English already hold all of northern France, and if they manage to break this mighty stronghold, the gateway to southern France will be laid open for them as well. Surely the

Dauphin couldn't survive such a defeat! As I speak, the English forces are on red alert in their garrisons, and reinforcements are on their way. There really isn't time for any arguing among the French commanders – but that's exactly what happened here earlier on today. The famous young visionary, Joan, was under the impression that the French forces would attack the English straight away. When the Duke of Alençon and Captain la Hire explained that the first priority was somehow to get relief supplies into the city, Joan was reportedly furious. People have told me she was even more angry when she realised that the advice of her voices had been ignored. Apparently Joan shouted, 'You KNEW my voices told us to go in from the north! So why are we approaching from the south?' I myself then witnessed one of the many miracles which seem to accompany this young girl wherever she goes. The French tried to set the supply boats afloat to sail them up the river and into the city, but the wind was set dead against them. Joan prayed for a while and all at once the wind totally changed direction. The boats sailed right into the city as if God himself was blowing into the sails. On that bombshell, it's back to the studio...

29 April 1429

Here I am INSIDE the city of Orléans. Today has been an amazing day for the French forces. Who would have believed last night that the French soldiers would take just one day to enter a city that has been besieged for more than six months! But everyone I have spoken to here agrees that it was Joan and the wind change that made it happen. Everyone saw the miracle yesterday, and from that moment on, the mood in both camps completely changed. Here among the French, the commanders stopped arguing and began to take Joan's voices more seriously. The soldiers were inspired with new hope and courage. They really believe that Joan has been sent by God and that God will grant them victory. On the other hand, the English have obviously been terrified out of their wits by Joan and her amazing powers. This evening, when Joan led the French soldiers towards Orléans and right into the city, the English didn't even make a move to stop them. Joan has literally 'put the fear of God' into the enemies of France...

4 May 1429

Several important garrisons defending Orléans remain to be taken from the English. However, there was an important French victory today, here at the Fort St Loup. Once again, it was all due to the amazing young girl the English are now calling a witch – Joan the Maid. According to Joan's squire, she took a rest in the afternoon with strict instructions to the other French commanders to wake her if they decided to attack. Once again, the captains overruled the Maid and let her sleep on. When several French regiments had gone into battle and the fighting was well underway, Joan suddenly sprang up from her sleep, crying, 'My voices have told me they have gone to attack the English!' Apparently, she was in such a hurry to put her armour on and dash outside that she forgot her standard, and her squire had to pass it out to her through the window. The Maid made it to the battlefield just in time to save the French from defeat at the hands of English reinforcements. It seems that whenever the young country girl-turned-knight is on the battlefield, the French can do no wrong.

7 May 1429

Today I am outside the garrison Les Tourelles, with Joan's priest, Father Jean Pasquerel. Father, can you tell us about the Maid's latest prediction, please?

"Well, yesterday evening a very worried Joan told me that she was going to be wounded by an arrow in the chest."

Thank you, Father. Viewers, I can confirm that in the fighting today, Joan was indeed wounded by an arrow in the chest. I myself saw it happen. The injury would have prevented an ordinary knight from taking any further part in the fighting. But I can tell you that after a few prayers, the Maid was up again, inspiring the French and petrifying the English with her astounding recovery. Furthermore, as the English captain Glasdale was trying to retreat over the bridge, it collapsed under him. He and all his soldiers fell into the moat and were drowned. All the talk in the English camp tonight is of how the 'witch' Joan healed herself by magic and used her powers to deliberately collapse the bridge. However, nothing can dampen the French high spirits. They are more convinced than ever that the Maid is an agent of God.

8 May 1429

Tonight, the sound you can hear in the background is the ringing of church bells – a noise that has not been heard in Orléans since the start of the siege nearly seven months ago.

For today, the French have finally won control of the city from the English! Joan now has approval at the highest levels of French society. The Archbishop of Embrun told me earlier that 'God has chosen a little flea to work for him and alight on the dunghill of France'. Now I'm off to join in the celebrations and it's back to the studio...

12 June 1429

You can see behind me the town of Jargeau, where today another English-occupied fortress fell into the hands of the French. However, as usual, the main talk tonight is not of the continuing French victories but of the Maid, Joan. Today, she was struggling up a siege ladder while bravely carrying her standard, when an English soldier threw a rock that struck her hard on the head. It knocked her right off the siege ladder and sent her tumbling into the ditch far below. Joan lay motionless

for several minutes, and the news spread like wildfire that she was dead. However, no sooner had the English started to celebrate than Joan was up on her feet shouting, 'Forward! Forward! God says the town is ours!' The English were so startled at the reappearance of the girl they call 'the witch' that they completely went to pieces. Every last English soldier was killed...

18 June 1429

Yet another of the Maid's predictions came true here today, at Patay. According to my sources, the Duke of Alençon asked Joan for her voices' advice on how the French should attack. Joan told him to 'use his spurs'. At first, everyone thought the Maid meant that the French should give up and gallop away. However, she corrected their mistake with a laugh and told everyone that by the end of the day, they'd be chasing the English as they fled. I can confirm that it all happened exactly as Joan said...

July 1429

Joan and her forces have now arrived here, in Troyes. Before the townspeople had met the Maid for themselves, some of them had begun to believe the English rumours about Joan being a witch. I have with me Brother Richard, who was sent out by the authorities to greet Joan and check whether or not she was good or evil. Brother Richard, can you tell me in your own words what happened, please?

"Well, having heard all about the Maid and her strange powers, I was extremely nervous about meeting her, I can tell you. I went out prepared with buckets of holy water and my best large cross, all ready to drive the devil out of her. However, Joan didn't seem at all bothered by the fact that I suspected she might be a witch. She just laughed and said, 'Don't worry, I won't fly off!' Rather embarrassing for me really. Actually, except for dressing like a man and praying rather a lot, Joan seems to me to be perfectly normal."

Thank you, Brother Richard. And I have some EXCLUSIVE news for our viewers tonight. Sources very close to Joan have told me that she has never killed a single soul. She acts fearlessly in battle, leading assaults on the enemy and carrying her standard into the thick of the fighting. However, she has never laid a hand on a single soldier and often weeps at the sight of the injured and dying – the English as well as the French. Viewers, we'll of course keep you updated with any new details about this extraordinary young prophetess just as soon as we have any...

17 July 1429

Today was the day that most people thought would never come. Charles the Dauphin was anointed with holy oil and crowned King of France here at Rheims Cathedral. Joan the Maid was at his side with her standard – she said it had seen the suffering, so it was only right that it should see the glory too. Experts have noted that two of the prophecies Joan made to the university panel at Poitiers have now come true. Tonight, everyone is asking themselves whether it's only a matter of time before the remaining two prophecies come true, too. Joan the Maid is the talk of France...

August 1429

Joan-mania has hit an all-time high. The public is flocking to see her wherever she goes. They bring her sick babies to cure, and try to kiss her feet, touch her rings and rip off bits of her clothes as relics. The men and women of France are literally expecting miracles. They are making medals with Joan's face on and putting her picture up in churches, and generally treating the Maid like a living saint. Things are getting quite out of control. Some priests disapprove of it all very strongly. Even Joan herself doesn't like it! She refuses to attempt to cure people and tries to keep out of the limelight as much as possible. On top of all this bother, sources close to the Maid have told me that she is very frustrated by the new king's lack of action. Now Charles has been crowned, he doesn't seem to want to bother to order any further fighting. And as Joan has so often been heard to say, 'God helps those who help themselves'...

8 September 1429

At last Joan was today back in action on the battlefield, trying to take Paris back from the English. It was the first time the French forces had tried to take a major enemy stronghold since Charles's coronation. But today the tide of the war seems to have turned. The Maid and her army have today tasted the bitterness of a shock defeat. Tonight the English are rejoicing and the French are horrorstruck. Joan's critics are gloating, saying that the witch's magic has finally failed. They have

pointed out that Joan shouldn't have chosen Our Lady's birthday on which to mount a major attack. Joan herself has refused to say that God has let her down. Instead, she has put the failure down to her own impatience. The Maid has let it be known that she went ahead without the approval of her voices, so it was her own mistake...

November 1429

There have been reports of many prophetesses in France since Joan first became famous, and today the Maid came face to face with one of them – a woman called Catherine de la Rochelle. Catherine told Joan that a white lady dressed in gold appeared to her every night and told her to travel through France trying to raise funds for the army – which is just what

Joan herself is doing at the moment. Joan wanted to see Catherine's vision for herself. After all, the Maid's own visions are so real that she actually touches them. And on just two occasions, it has been rumoured that other people have shared her visions with her. So the Maid stayed awake all night with Catherine – and didn't see a thing, even though Catherine insisted that the white lady came. Catherine was none too pleased that Joan didn't believe her story...

April 1430

Joan recently caused quite a stir when she prayed inside this very church for a baby that had stopped breathing and looked as black as death. The Maid's prayers brought it back to life just long enough for it to be baptised, so even though it died again, it could at least be buried in holy ground. However, I have to report that not everyone approves of Joan. Last week, the Maid did a deal to swap an English prisoner of war, Francquet Arras, for a French prisoner of war. However, today she found out that the French prisoner of war had died, so there was no one to swap Arras with. As Arras was a confessed murderer, the Maid had him executed instead. Immediately, some critics have accused the Maid of going against the code of chivalry by executing a prisoner she had already agreed to ransom. Controversy surrounds the Maid and is growing day by day...

23 May 1430

Today has been a disastrous day for the French. The unthinkable has happened. Joan the Maid has been captured! The French were attacking Compiègne, and while Joan was leading a brave charge, a Burgundian archer got close enough to her to grab hold of her cloak and drag her off her horse. I have been talking to the devastated French soldiers and can report that some of them think she was betrayed by her own people. They have told me that they think Joan was deliberately abandoned to the enemy by La Tremoille – after all, La Tremoille was King Charles's chief adviser until Joan came along and he has reportedly always been extremely jealous of her. Some of the French soldiers I have interviewed reckon that La Tremoille ordered one of his henchmen to lock Joan and her troops

outside the castle when most of the French had already retreated safely inside. I have been unable to find out whether this accusation is true or not. However, one thing is for certain: the country girl's courtly clothes were certainly part of the reason why she has come a cropper!

CHAPTER SIX

A Dirty Dungeon and a Dismal Death

Whether you were a prisoner of war or just a plain criminal, it wasn't pleasant being a captive in medieval times. For a start, dungeons were damp, freezing, stinking, rat-infested stone pits – often without a single window to let in any light and little drainage to let out the sewage. Worst of all were 'oubliettes' – tiny holes deep underground into which the worst prisoners were thrown and just forgotten about.

Then there was torture. You could be stretched out on a machine called the 'rack' until your tendons snapped and your bones popped out of their sockets. You could have your thumbs squashed in thumbscrews, or your foot crushed in a contraption called the 'boot'. You could have your tongue ripped out of your mouth by a vicious iron tongue-twister. You could be hung from the ceiling in iron clamps – either around your wrists, or worse, around your feet, so you were left dangling upside down! And the torturers had many more ideas up their sleeves...

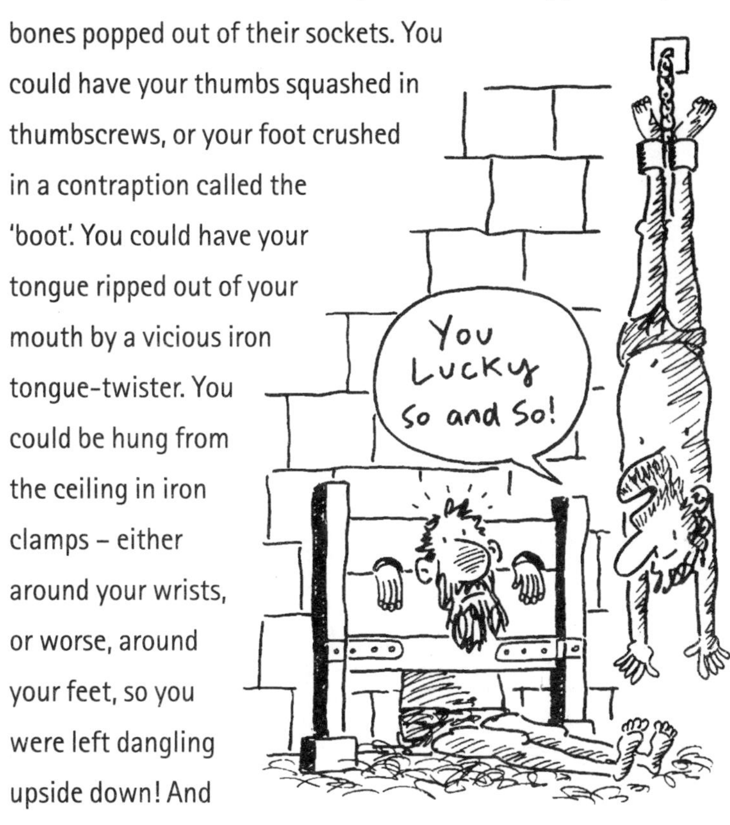

Worst of all, medieval people were so into cruel punishments that if you were put on trial, you didn't stand much of a chance of being found not guilty – even if you really WERE innocent!

A CLOSE SHAVE AND A NARROW SQUEAK

With Joan's reputation for magic, her guards must have been expecting her to disappear into thin air at any minute – which is in fact, what she very nearly did! As a special prisoner, they held her in solitary confinement. Joan was first kept in the tower of a château, with guards posted outside her room. In the middle of the night, the determined girl managed to remove enough of the planks in the floor to slip down silently into the unlocked room beneath. She got as far as the main entrance before the night patrol noticed her and raised the alarm!

After that, Joan was held in another tower. She very nearly vanished from that, too! Joan jumped out of a window in an attempt to escape. It was a very long way down – 18 metres, to be precise. She didn't exactly make a good landing either – those who found her thought she was dead. But once again, it didn't take her long to make a miraculous recovery.

OUT OF THE FRYING PAN, INTO THE FIRE

In November 1430, a deal was done to hand Joan over to her

worst enemies – the English, who clapped her in irons and locked her into a cell in Rouen with the roughest soldiers they could find to 'guard' her (more like torment and harrass her). By the way, I hope you've noticed by now that the ungrateful Charles the Dauphin hadn't made a single attempt to rescue Joan, or even made an offer to ransom her – which was nearly always done, and for far lesser knights than Joan.

Unfortunately, the Catholic church had gradually become more and more suspicious about Joan's voices, visions and so-called 'miracles'. An official church court assembled (called the Inquisition), and over 170 judges began to question Joan to find out if they could charge her with the crimes of being a witch and a heretic (someone who refused to submit to the authority of the church). In those days they could arrest you, interrogate you and torture you first, with a view to charging you later – which was again bad luck if you hadn't in fact done anything wrong.

HUBBLE, BUBBLE, TOIL AND TROUBLE

The Inquisition wanted to give Joan as many bad marks as possible and ultimately find her guilty. There were several reasons why...

- The English hated Joan. They felt she had single-handedly turned the tide of the war against them and caused them to lose several important cities – not to mention hundreds of troops. **Ten out of ten bad marks for this one.**

- The church representatives were extremely niggled by the way Joan wore male clothes – and such fine, luxurious ones, too. They accused her of 'having cast aside all womanly decency'. But what niggled the grand, educated churchmen even more was that the simple peasant girl refused to do what they said and put a dress back on. Well, they couldn't be having teenage rebels going around defying the church, could they? Firstly, it made Joan a heretic. And secondly, it made them look very stupid. **So ten out of ten bad marks for that, too.**

- Medieval people lived in terror of those who were in league with the devil – witches and sorcerers who practised black magic. When a suspected devil-worshipper died, people cut off their right hand in the belief that this would undo the spells they had cast. And it wasn't just your average medieval peasant who thought this way. In 1326 Pope John XXII confirmed everyone's fears when he gave the church the official power to seek out witches and sorcerers and get rid of them. Only 63 years after Joan's death, witch-hunting had become such big business that two church Inquisitors wrote a book of instructions (called the *Malleus Maleficarum*) on how to do it properly as a full-time career! Joan was in trouble because the English had from the very start declared that her strange powers weren't from God – they were witchcraft. (After all, Joan wasn't on their side, was she?) The especially bad news for Joan was that medieval people believed the devil could appear in any shape or form – even in the disguise of something heavenly! Once Joan had followed up her great victories with a few lost battles, people began to think that her voices and visions were highly suspect – and she could do nothing to prove her own belief that they were genuinely holy. **Eleven out of ten bad marks for this one.**

THE END IS NIGH

After four months solid of intense, hostile questioning, the Inquisition found Joan guilty as charged. On the threat of torture they ordered her to recant, which means going back on your word and saying you've made everything up. The church firstly wanted Joan to say that she didn't believe her voices and visions came from God after all. And secondly, that she'd do what they wanted and wear women's clothes. (She'd always insisted that she couldn't, because God had told her that he wanted her to dress like a man.) It seems that, for fear of being burnt alive, poor Joan admitted to all the church's accusations. However, some people say she was tricked into signing a confession – remember, she couldn't read, and she can't have been feeling on top form after all that time in an enemy prison, either.

By recanting, Joan had escaped burning. But she was horrified at the sentence that was meted out to her instead. She was ordered to put on women's clothing and condemned to be kept in solitary confinement for the rest of her life – and not even in a church prison, as was usual in this sort of case, but in a normal English prison. Within four days, Joan had changed her mind. She put on her men's clothing again and vowed that everything she had ever said was true. Moreover, Joan announced that her voices said she had greatly displeased God by saying that they had never existed. On 30 May 1431, Joan was led out to be burnt at the stake.

AN EVENTFUL EXECUTION

Joan never gave up her belief in God and that she had done what he wanted. And for some reason, her captors showed her some mercy and allowed her to see a priest for a last Mass – which they hadn't done all the time she was in prison. (This was especially strange because the church didn't allow recognised sinners to take Holy Communion.) While the flames licked around her body and the smoke curled upwards, Joan cried out repeatedly to Jesus, Mary and the saints. She asked for a crucifix and an Englishman hurried to make her one out of a few scraps of wood and held it up on a pole so she could see it. It took a long time for Joan to die, because the fire had been specially prepared to give her a slow, painful death.

There were several reports of strange things that happened when Joan died:

- One of the executioners is thought to have seen a white dove flying up out of the flames. Apparently he said: 'I greatly fear that I am damned, for I have burnt a holy woman.'

- Another person said that he saw the word 'Jesus' written in the flames.

- Several said that Joan's heart never burned away – even though sulphur and oil were poured on the fire in an attempt to set it alight.

Lastly, Joan's ashes were finally thrown into the river – firstly, so they couldn't be buried on holy ground, and secondly, so that no one could use her relics either in holy rituals or black magic. And that was an end to the matter... or so the Inquisition thought.

AFTERWORD

Sorry! We made a mistake

Just like Elvis, Joan had become a legend in her own lifetime. In an age when there was no e-mail, telephone, TV, radio, newspapers or postal service – and when most people couldn't read or write anyway – Joan grew to be famous far and wide in a very short space of time (she was in the public eye for no more than three years). She was gossiped about on both sides of the English Channel by thousands of people who had never met her, as well as those who had. So many rumours went flying around about her that people were fascinated by her – even though they found it hard to know what was the truth and what was exaggerated or even totally made-up. Everyone wasn't going to forget about Joan that easily!

Some people were keen to believe that Joan was still alive – so keen that rumours soon went round that someone else had been burned at the stake in her place! These were made worse by the fact that false 'Joans' started to pop up all over the place, in an attempt to cash in on her fame.

Those who were more sensible and realised that Joan really was dead, straight away began to feel rather guilty and wonder whether she had been innocent after all.

- In 1450, when Charles had recaptured Paris and was well on his way to driving out the English (just as Joan had predicted), he opened a half-hearted enquiry into his heroine's trial.

- In 1452, even the church itself wondered whether it might have done the wrong thing and ruled that Joan's case should be re-opened.

- A proper investigation took place between 1455 and 1456 and the verdict of 'guilty' was overturned. Justice at last! But a bit late for poor Joan...

- In 1920, the Catholic church made Joan a saint. (Mind you, it took them long enough to get round to it!)

Today, Joan is admired as one of the national heroes of France – and after all that, rightly so, wouldn't you think?

Timeline

1412 Joan of Arc is born.

1422 August – Henry V of England dies. His son, Henry, is proclaimed king of England and France. Charles the Dauphin also proclaims himself king of France.

1422 October – Mad King Charles VI of France dies.

1425 13-year-old Joan sees her first vision in her village church at Domrémy.

1429 Joan travels to see Charles the Dauphin at the royal court of Chinon. Charles sets tests for her, which she passes, and she is then fully-equipped as a knight.

1429 April to July – Siege of Orléans. Joan leads French army in successful defence of the city.

1429 July 17th – Charles the Dauphin anointed as king of France at Rheims cathedral.

1429 September 8th – Joan loses battle trying to take back Paris from the English.

1430 Joan continues to see visions and use her powers of healing.

1430 April – Controversy surrounding Joan and her powers grows. Some see her as a witch.

1430 May 23rd – French attack Compiègne. Joan is captured.

1430 November – Deal is done to hand over Joan to the English. She is imprisoned in Rouen.

1431 Spring – Joan is tried and found guilty.

1431 May 30th – Joan of Arc is burnt at the stake.

1450 Charles now opens an enquiry into Joan's trial.

1452 The Church orders Joan's case to be re-opened.

1456 Investigation into trial – 'guilty' verdict is overturned.

1920 Catholic Church makes Joan a saint.

titles in the series

Spilling the Beans on Julius Caesar

Spilling the Beans on Shakespeare

Spilling the Beans on Tutankhamen

Spilling the Beans on Einstein

Spilling the Beans on Napoleon

Spilling the Beans on Robin Hood

Spilling the Beans on Buffalo Bill

Spilling the Beans on Marie Antoinette

Spilling the Beans on Boudicca

Spilling the Beans on Joan of Arc